# Welcome to Space Camp

by Mary Kate O'Day

PEARSON

Scott
Foresman

Editorial Offices: Glenview, Illinois • Parsippany, New Jersey • New York, New York
Sales Offices: Needham, Massachusetts • Duluth, Georgia • Glenview, Illinois
Coppell, Texas • Sacramento, California • Mesa, Arizona

Astronauts weigh less on the Moon, so they bounce as they walk.

In July 1969, three astronauts traveled to the Moon. Two of the astronauts, Neil Armstrong and Buzz Aldrin, walked on the Moon. The other astronaut, Michael Collins, circled the Moon in the spacecraft.

Alone in space, Neil and Buzz landed their tiny lunar module on the Moon. There were rocks everywhere. Since there is no air on the Moon, there was no wind. They felt lighter than on Earth. Their first job was to learn to walk on the Moon.

---

**spacecraft:** a vehicle used for flight in space; spaceship

Today, spaceships go far beyond the Moon. But before spacecraft could travel into space, scientists had to find a way to escape Earth's gravity.

space shuttle

rockets

Rockets help spacecraft escape Earth's gravity.

## Did You Know?  Gravity

Gravity is a force that draws or pulls smaller objects toward larger objects in space. Gravity keeps the Moon traveling around Earth in an orbit. On Earth, gravity pulls objects and people toward the center of the Earth.

So how does anything ever leave Earth? Spacecraft use powerful rockets to escape Earth's gravity.

---

**orbit:** a circular or an egg-shaped path that one object follows around another object

**rockets:** machines that use fuel and gas to force a spacecraft upward into space

Would you like to enjoy an astronaut's experience without leaving Earth? You can do it at a space camp.

Astronauts need to prepare before they go on a space flight. To prepare themselves, they do simulation activities. At space camp, you will do simulation activities, too. But first, you will need to prepare for them. You will begin by watching demonstrations. You will play games and do experiments with other campers.

After that, you will be ready to try out the same simulation activities astronauts do to prepare for space travel. These simulations let you experience what astronauts feel in space.

---

**simulation activities:** activities like those done in space

Astronauts spend many months preparing for space travel. They do activities that simulate work in space.

A simulator is a piece of equipment that lets astronauts practice the things they need to do in space. Astronauts must learn to stay alive in space where there is no air to breathe. They take air with them from Earth. They have to learn how to move in space. They have to learn how to work in space. They have to learn how to eat and sleep in space.

There is very little gravity in a spaceship. Astronauts float in the air. During simulation activities, astronauts learn to work while floating.

---

**simulate:** act like; pretend to be like

5

At space camp, campers use simulators like those used by astronauts.

Astronauts must learn to walk, work, sleep, and eat in zero gravity. Food floats in the air. Sometimes astronauts have to catch it to eat it. Sometimes they squeeze their food out of a tube, right into their mouth!

At space camp, you practice doing things in zero gravity. At some camps you can use a 1/6th gravity chair. In the 1/6th gravity chair, you will feel like you are walking on the moon.

In a weightlessness simulator, you will float and walk as you would float and walk in space. You feel weightless—as if you weight nothing. These are some of the simulators you can use at camp.

_____

**zero gravity:** condition of weightlessness

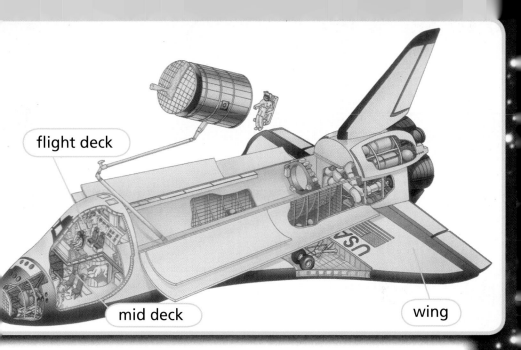

flight deck

mid deck

wing

Diagram of a space shuttle

Your space camp may have a full-scale copy of a space shuttle. A space shuttle is a reusable spacecraft with wings. The wings let astronauts control the landing on Earth. You can climb aboard the replica and work inside it.

Inside the replica, you will explore the flight deck where the astronauts control the spacecraft. You will see the mid deck where much of the other work is done. As you explore the decks, you will learn about the many jobs an astronaut has to do in space.

---

**full-scale:** same size as the original

**reusable:** able to be used again and again

**replica:** copy

Sometimes campers can experience a space mission. During this part of space camp you work in teams of six.

One team works in the control center outside the shuttle. This team is like the team of scientists who stay on Earth during a real mission to space. Their work is just as important as the work of the astronauts in the spacecraft. These scientists control many of the things that happen in space during a mission.

The other team works inside the shuttle. They use the controls, make decisions, and follow orders.

---

**mission:** trip with a goal or a job to do

The teams do everything that must be done on a real mission. They must launch the spacecraft and put it into orbit. Every real mission to space has experiments and other jobs to do. So the teams do jobs and experiments to learn about the universe and outer space.

There is a lot of work to do in the control center, too. The teams must work together to get the shuttle safely back to Earth. The jobs require teamwork. That is why astronauts finish the workshops and use the simulators before going into space. Everything they learn is used during the mission into space.

---

**universe:** everything that exists everywhere, even in outer space

A multimedia production uses sound, images, and sometimes actors.

At some space camps, you can see rockets and spacecraft used by real astronauts in space. At other space camps, you will study a model of the solar system—our sun and its planets. You may learn the history of space exploration in a movie or a multimedia production. You probably will learn about Galileo and Newton—two men who explored space from Earth long ago.

At space camp, you will learn to sleep and eat as you would in space. You may eat freeze-dried space food.

Space camps let you try many different activities. Some camps let you build and launch a small rocket. At other camps, you can build and operate a robot. You may learn how to stay alive or perform experiments. All these activities let you feel what it is like to be an astronaut in space.

---

**freeze-dried:** food from which all the water has been removed by freezing

Do you think that it would be exciting to explore the whole universe? We cannot do that, but you can find out about it at space camp. Space camp can teach you about space exploration. Maybe one day, you will be an astronaut!